I AM POSITIVE

Living With a New Way of Thinking

Copyright © 2021 Antoinette Upchurch

This is a work of non-fiction. All rights reserved. No part of this book may be reproduced or transmitted in any form or by any means, electronic storage, and retrieval system, except in the case of brief quotations embodied in critical articles or reviews, without permission in writing from the publisher. In no way is it legal to reproduce, duplicate, or transmit any part of this document in either electronic means or in printed format. Recording of this publication is strictly prohibited and any storage of this document is not allowed unless with written permission from the publisher.

All rights reserved.

ISBN: 978-1-953760-03-6

Published by Pure Thoughts Publishing, LLC 2055 Gees Mill Rd #316 | Conyers, GA 30013 USA 470-440-0875 |
www.purethoughtspublishing.com

Printed in the United States of America

Table Of Contents

Introduction 5

Chapter 1
What are you thinking? 7

Chapter 2
Negative thoughts 10

Chapter 3
Stop thinking wrong 12

Chapter 4
Thinking positive in difficult times 17

Chapter 5
Change my thinking, change my Life! 21

Chapter 6
Focus on the good and not the bad 24

Chapter 7
The dangers of having the wrong thinking mentality 27

Chapter 8
The power of a renewed mind 30

Chapter 9
A New Way of Thinking 33

Chapter 10

    I am Positive 35

Chapter 11

    Daily Affirmations About Being Positive 38

About the Author 43

Introduction

I am writing this book to encourage those who may have faced times where it has been a struggle to be positive. I have learned that life comes with ups and downs, disappointments, emergencies, failures, mishaps, burdens, the good, the bad, and the ugly. I decided that I would not allow the negative to overtake me, but I begin to focus on the positive. Once I began to focus on the positive, I began to see my life from a different perspective. I concluded that the negative situations in my life required me to face them with a positive mindset. I began to say to myself, "No matter how negative things seem in my life I will focus on remaining positive." I have learned so many lessons from my life, and now I understand that I have a right to make my life better by changing my mentality about the way I see life outcomes.

This book will be used to motive and encourage people to focus on the positive. I do realize that it is hard to always think positive when the world has changed in so many ways. I am very sympathetic to the fact that life's challenges sometimes bring challenges and hopelessness. But this is the opportunity for us to begin to see ourselves overcoming our challenges and see ourselves being positive about our situation. I got tired of living in fear and feeling nothing would ever change for me. I began to pray and ask God to help me change the way I see myself when I am in a negative situation. I had to ask God to allow me to become an optimist instead of a pessimist. If situations in my life were negative, then I focused on nothing good happening. I had to change and began to speak positively about my life even when it looked the total opposite of what I spoke. This book is about me and how I struggled with being negative, but I overcame it. I am now living with a new way of being and thinking because *I AM POSITIVE*!

Chapter 1

What are you thinking?

I had to ask myself what I was thinking; and why was I thinking that way. I began to take a deep look at myself and faced the fact that being negative had become a way of life for me. I had to say to myself, Antoinette you have a negative mindset. My mindset was not to see anything positive come out of my situations in life, but for me to only focus on the way things look and not believing that it could change. I knew in my heart that my mindset needed to change, but at this point, it was more comfortable for me to stay in the posture of being negative. Being negative was easy for me because bad things always grabbed my attention first. I knew that negativism made it easy for me to complain, be frustrated, give up, and having feelings that nothing is going to ever get better for me.

As I look back, I realized that anytime I encountered negative situations in my life, I only focused on a negative outcome. I remember one time the doctor requested me to get a blood test done to check on my liver enzymes, and the first thing after the blood test I began to allow fear to set in and I begin to think wrong. I promise you for two days I set around worrying and feeling that everything was going to go wrong with the test. Honestly, I could hear the still small voice of God telling me to believe the worst. I knew that being a Christian I should not have been thinking this way, but a part of me wanted to believe my blood work report would be negative. So, the third day came, and I had not heard from the doctor and my mind was really thinking wrong. I remember standing up in my kitchen and saying to myself, "Antoinette what in the world are you thinking?" So, I began to talk to myself and tell myself to stop those negative thoughts. I remember picking up the Bible and turning to Philippians 4: 8th verse: Finally, brethren, whatsoever things are honest, whatsoever things are just, whatsoever things are pure, whatsoever things are lovely, whatsoever things are of a good report; if there be any virtue, and if there be any praise, think on these things. That scripture began to convict me because I realized right then and there I was not thinking about good things. I needed to change my thinking and then I could change what I was focusing on. At that minute I opened my mouth and began to pray and talk to God about my issue. I cried out and said God I need your help. I cannot change this about myself, but only you can. I then began to take responsibility and began to challenge myself to think positively about my blood work. The next morning, I received a call and the nurse confirmed that my blood work was good. I knew then that I was going to need an overhaul in my thought mentality. I could make excuses for myself but there was no point in doing that. I knew then that as a believer of God I needed to change my thinking and it was going to take some time, but I realized that I had to start today. Remember starting something today means you are willing to start somewhere. I began to be positive and repeat to myself that change is a process so I may as well start today. God did not design for me to live my life from a negative standpoint, but he wants me to get the best out of my life, and grow and be the best me I can be. I wanted to begin to see myself the way God sees me. I had to realize that God has great plans for me; and that he is not thinking evil towards me. So, from then on, I worked on changing my thought mentality; and focusing on thinking positive and not negative. I would ask myself this question: What are you thinking about the situation. I knew I must face the truth about the situation, and that I could expect a good outcome. Even if the outcome is not the best, I still wanted to have good energy about the situation and not allow my mind to lead me into being anxious and upset. So, I began to hang on to the fact that if I change my thinking, I can change my life. I want my thinking to line up with the words of my mouth, and then my words can catapult my life in the right direction.

Chapter 2

Negative thoughts

When I was thinking about my thoughts, I want my thoughts to be conducive to what is good for me. Webster's dictionary defines thoughts as: an individual's act or product of thinking. Dictionary.com gave these synonyms for the word thought: thinking, understanding and reflection. I really like these definitions because they describe thoughts to a good point. Understanding what thoughts are and how to redirect my mind when I am thinking negatively. Thoughts will always come into our mind because the brain consists of a continuation of thinking.

There are times when good and bad thoughts will come to mind, but what do we do with our thoughts. Our thoughts can affect the way we perceive things. Negative thoughts can come from what we have been through whether good or bad. All people have struggles, tragedies, and disappointments; and I understand how that feels because I have been through all three. When I was bombarded with life stressors, I had to consciously try to manage my thoughts regarding whatever the stressor was. It is easy for the mind to think about what is negative versus the positive. When negative thoughts would enter my mind, it would sound like things are not going to turn out right, this is bad, things always go wrong for you and look at this situation is not getting any better. Well, guess what? I had to stop the thought in midair and change the way I was thinking at that time. Negative thoughts can derail you from staying positive. I knew I needed to practice being healthy every day. Negative thoughts are consuming, weighty, burdensome, challenging, irritating, and opposing. Negative thoughts can produce fear and worry. There is a scripture in the Bible that blesses me when negative thoughts come to mind. The scripture is 2nd Corinthians 10:5 Casting down imaginations, and every high thing that exalted itself against the knowledge of God and bringing into captivity every thought to the obedience of Christ; and having a readiness to revenge all disobedience when your obedience is fulfilled. In other words, I can take my thoughts captive by simply gaining control over what I am thinking. I realized that whatever I think in my mind could possibly have a positive or negative effect on me. I am now a recipient of whatever I am thinking. I decided to focus my thoughts on the right stuff! Thoughts are immensely powerful, and they will and can change the way you see your life if you let them. I came to grips that I had to begin to stop the thoughts that I was thinking because the negative thoughts were beginning to shape my world, and this was not good at all!

Chapter 3

Stop thinking wrong

This is one of the most important chapters in the book because I had to make the choice to stop thinking long and wrong. I went through a period in my life where fear had gripped me, and it made me think wrong about my life situations. Fear paralyzed my thoughts to the point that everything I went through I looked at it wrong. If something came up in my life and I had no control over it fear would jump on me and I began to feel I could do nothing to change my situation. What did fear look like in my life? Fear looked like failure, defeat, hopelessness, stress, giving up, death, depression, and pessimism. I can say this because this is about what I went through. I am a very transparent person to some degree, and I just want to be real with you about my experience. I had to realize that everyone is not the same. I finally face the fact that I had a lot of negativity attached to me because I was afraid. What is fear? According to Webster's Dictionary fear is defined as an unpleasant often strong emotion caused by anticipation or awareness of danger and being anxious. Thesaurs.com used these words to describe fear: anxiety, dismay, doubt, horror, jitters, and unease. Fear played a huge place in my life by making me feel very anxious all the time. I got tired of feeling anxious. My negative thoughts were not only dominating my mind, but my conversations with people released a vibe of being negative about everything. As a child of God, I realized that I could have breakdowns in my life. I had several overwhelming periods in my life, and I am not ashamed to share them. One of my breakdowns occurred when I was in my late 20's and early 30's. I realized then that I did not face issues from my childhood. I went through things in my childhood that made me fearful as an adult. I was very pessimistic because of the level of dysfunction in my home when I was young. I tended to see life negatively, all my conversations were negative and after a while, it began to make me sick physically. I was feeling drained from living with fear and being negative. I developed high blood pressure, anxiety disorder and depression because I was constantly worrying and being fearful. My spiritual life was not as strong as it should be. I was speaking God's Word, but I was not truly applying the Word of God to situations in my life. I realized that I needed to renew my mind and change the way I was thinking. I began to take cognitive responsibility and note that I needed to change my mentality and speech as related to how I was dealing with my life. ***I was thinking long, but I was thinking wrong.*** I realized it was my time to make a change. Mentally, I was drained, and I was taking medication and seeing a Christian therapist. God used my Christian therapist to help me work on redirecting my thoughts and changing the way I was processing my life's situations. My therapist also encouraged me to use the Word of God as compassion and not from a place of God being angry with me because I was mentally drained. That alone was a religious and self-righteous thought to think God was angry with me because I was mentally drained. I began working on changing my mentality right then and there. My therapist was one of the people God used to help me understand that God loves me, and he wants the best for me. I began to look at my life to see what I needed to begin to have the mind of Christ concerning situations in my life. I took this one scripture and meditated on it for days, weeks, and months. The Bible says in Philippians 2: 5, "Let this mind be in you which was also in Christ Jesus!" I began to ask myself how would Jesus think? I also read Ephesians 4:23-24vs. which says, be renewed in the spirit of your mind; and that ye put on the new man, which after God is created in righteousness and true holiness. I realized there was a renewal of mind that God wanted to give me. But being renewed in my mind would have to truly become a way of living; and continually building up that new person to go along with my new life. I knew then that my mind would have to be refurbished every day. I also recognized that my way of thinking had to change for me to become a new person. I was so relieved to know that I did not have to live a miserable life and that I can change the way I see my situation no matter how bad it was. I began to redirect my thoughts when they were not positive. I knew that I would be faced with negative things again and again but how I process my thoughts about the situation would determine my level of mental stability. One thing I was sure of was that I am positive about being positive! I had to believe that God has great things in store for me. I needed to take on a positive attitude. I knew that God was not happy about me emotionally drained nor being mentally tormented by my negative thoughts. I had to begin to cast down those negative thoughts and begin to see things from a different perspective. I began to work on my thoughts by reading the Word of God and using it to help process situations in my life. I deliberately began to work on my thinking and did it for years and I continue to do it now. I made my mind up that when those same thoughts try to come back, I will not think wrong I will think strong! I will allow the Holy Spirit to arise in my life and give me the peace and understanding that I need for the situation.

God did not create me to think wrong. God wants me to think strong and know that God has good thoughts about me. So, if God has good thoughts about me then I need to have good thoughts about my own situation. My life was changing, and I knew I had to be ready for the punches and curves that were coming my way. I needed to change my thinking because the Bible says in Proverbs 23: 7 For as a man thinketh in his heart, so is he. I realized I could be saying positive things with my mouth, but my heart was in a completely different place. I to made sure my mind and heart lined up together. Negativity could no longer live in my heart if I were to survive in this life. Every day, I worked to make sure that I was thinking right, talking right, and doing right. I did this change for myself and not for anyone else, I knew my husband and children needed me to change and I did. But I had to realize that I was addicted to being negative. Now it irritates me when I hear negative talkers, but I am patient with them, and I realize it took time for me to change too. I am better for it right now. I knew that thinking wrong does not make you strong. I repented to God for being a negative person with multiple complaints and not wanting to take responsibility for my own shortcomings. I knew then that this change looked good on me; and that God wanted me to be set free from the torments of the mind. So, periodically over the years when I battled with negative thoughts, I went back to when God first changed me and help me to get myself together as related to my thoughts. I am still using my formula that if you think wrong, you will not be strong. I am on the path of thinking about what is conducive for the healthiness of my life. I am staying focused, and I realized, "I am Positive!"

Chapter 4

Thinking positive in difficult times

The pandemic really changed our world and we all have had to deal with a world filled with uncertainty. The pandemic produced a lot of panic, unsettledness, fear, and doubt. The pandemic impacted jobs changed the economic system and health status of many people; and the educational systems had to make major changes to accommodate students. During this time, the pandemic created an exceedingly difficult time for our family. Our family had to deal with the fact that my husband's mom contracted Covid-19 and she passed away. It was so hard for my husband because when he visited his mom at the rehabilitation center he could never go in and see her in person; he had to visit his mom at her bedroom window. The last time we visited my mother-in-law my husband and I knew that something was different about her. This was a tough time for our family. Remaining positive was extremely hard to do, but we plowed through and did it. My husband has been holding on to the fact that his mom does not have to suffer from pain anymore, yet we miss her.

I faced a major difficulty and I never thought it would happen to me. One morning I awoke, and I went to the bathroom, and I was bleeding. I knew in my heart something was wrong because I was menopausal and bleeding at this time was not a good sign. Thoughts began to take over my mind, and I had to reframe my thoughts and tell myself not to speak anything negative over myself because I did not know what was going on with me. I called my gynecologist, and she called some medication in; and requested I come in two weeks later. I ended up calling her back and she requested I come in sooner. I began to talk to God and ask him to keep my thoughts positive about my situation. To make a long story short, my doctor did a biopsy in the office to see if there was any cancer present. Fortunately, the test came back negative, but she found a polyp growing in my uterus and I had to have surgery and be tested for endometrial cancer. I began to pray and admit to God that my human side began to kick in. I felt this was one of the most difficult things I had to face in life. I had not had the surgery and now am I walking around with this in my body. I wanted to get that foreign object out of me, and I was believing cancer was not involved. Just because I had one test in the office and passed another one, my doctor wanted to do another one to make I had no cancer. The appointment was set for my surgery; and it would be 21 days after the polyp was found in my uterus. I did not want to wait that long to have surgery, but I had no choice. During those 21 days my thoughts tried to consume me, but I continued to take control over my negative thoughts by giving everything to God. Every time a negative thought would come to my mind, I found myself reframing my what if this, and what if that. I spent a lot of time praying and reading my Bible. I distance myself from people because I did not want to hear anything negative. When fear would try to come to me, I would ask my husband, aunt and overseer for prayer. I also had another spiritual mother at that time that would call and encourage me too. Some of my close friends, family, and my spiritual sister Apostle G was always there to speak positiveness over me. My overseer reminded me that just because I was experiencing fear about my surgery and health this did not mean that I was not saved or weak; he reminded me that I was human. God began to touch and strengthen me during this time, and I began to change my thoughts and I reminded myself that according to 2nd Timothy 1:7 King James Version Bible it says, For God has not given us a spirit of fear; but of power, and love and a sound mind. I had to refocus my thoughts and reboot my spirit by remembering that I did not need to think negatively about my situation. I did not fear another minute, I just began to trust God to take care of me. But notice when you are facing difficult times you must stay focused, prayed up, hang around positive people and keep yourself in a place of peace. I did this and when surgery time came around, I trusted God. My family nor my husband could come into the surgical center with me because of the Covid rules. I was not happy about this at all, but my husband and his cousin set in the car in the parking lot waiting for me to go in and come out of surgery. Before surgery, my doctor, nurse and anesthesiologist came and talk to me, and I went into surgery and came out fine. I waited three days to get my test results and when I received my results there was no cancer found. I learned that difficult times would come, but how I was thinking about these times is what really counts. Even when I got a little discouraged and my thoughts tried to control me, I used right thinking to change my wrong thinking. I called and talked to positive people. I knew the outcome could possibly be bad, but God wanted me to stay positive and focus on a good outcome. At times it was hard and at the end of me waiting 21 days, God showed himself strong in my life. I had to concluded that I am Positive!

Chapter 5

Change my thinking, change my Life!

One thing I love about life is that I am free to make changes at any time. I like the fact that nothing has to stay the same. I knew that if change does not take place there is a possibility that my life could become even more complicated. After all my struggles, disappointment and realizing that thinking wrong and doing things my way was not working. I began to figure out quickly that I needed a positive lifestyle more than being miserable and looking at everything from a negative standpoint! I was so over the negative lifestyle. You may ask what my negative lifestyle was. My negative lifestyle was living my life thinking wrong every day, speaking wrong about my situation, complaining about everything, hanging around negative people and not trusting God the way I should have. I began to say to God, please overhaul my way of thinking, so I can think like you, Lord! I needed God to change my way of thinking. I wanted to make sure that I was giving God free reign in my life to do what He needed to do. I wanted to make sure that I was seeing life from a positive point. I realized that everyone I meet may not be into being positive all the time, but I had explained to them the way I used to think and now God has changed me. I want people to realize that when God changed me that he also changed my thinking. I knew I had nothing to prove to anybody, but it was best to let people know what I did not like upfront. What is change? Webster's dictionary defines change as becoming different; to undergo a transformation. Some synonyms for change according to Thesaurus.com: adjustments, transition, about-face, conversion, reversal, shift, and correction. All these words explained just what I had done as related to changing my way of changing. My relationship with God was not the same; and my thinking had changed a lot. God did not want me thinking wrong. I began to take note, that changing my thinking, had changed my life. I was thinking the way God designed; and now I was going to get the best out of my life as God had purposed for me. The same God that changed my mindset, is the same God that can change your mindset if you need to change and become more positive. My life had changed because now I was thinking the way God wanted me to. I realized that this new lifestyle of speaking positive was the key to catapulting my life in a new direction. There were no hold bars I was going to share my change with the world. I was so happy because I realized that I had changed my thinking; and my thinking had changed my life. Life is much better now that I have changed my thinking. I can face the most difficult situations from a different perspective. Perspective has a lot to do with how I saw the situation turning out. A negative perspective may produce a negative outcome. A positive perspective can produce a positive outcome. I had to ask myself which one I truly wanted. I already knew deep inside that I needed to be cognitive of how I looked at things. I made up in my mind that I was looking at myself and ready to change some things in my life. I was looking at myself doing better, being better and seeing myself being the person that God has destined for me to become. I knew then that life was going to be much better because I had overhauled my thinking and put a new perspective on how I seeing my situations. I realize then that there is a difference between changing and wanting to change my thinking. The right thinking in my life was going to produce better outcomes for me. This is the time when I must walk in total change and acceptance of what God is doing in my life. I am in awe of God's glory and change in my life because I am doing it his ways by focusing on changing my thinking. After all, it would make me a better person. I can truly say that I am positive!

There was a need for a mentality change as related to the way I was thinking. My thinking was considered stinking. I could not see anything good in what I was doing. No matter how good I was doing in life, I always expected something bad to happen. When I began to think positive, I began to feel good about myself and I could see myself overcoming and thinking right.

Chapter 6

Focus on the good and not the bad

Have you ever had to learn something quickly? I did. One thing I had to learn is to focus on the good and not the bad. It was not easy for me to do. I was so used to focusing on the bad because of the way I was thinking. Changing my mindset gave me the desire to focus on what is good. When I focus on good it makes me feel good. What happens when I focus? Vocabulary.com describes focus as when a person focuses on something it means they're paying attention to it. I had to pay attention to what I was thinking and why I was thinking it. I deliberately began to pay attention to my thoughts. I made sure that if I was facing something negative, then I would deliberately think positive about it. Being intentional about thinking good was vital for me when it came to be a positive thinker. I remember my grandma always saying that it is easier to focus on the bad instead of the good. I noticed that when I focused on bad things it made me feel bad; or even made me have anxiety about my situation. Feeling anxious is not a good way to live. I can remember the moment I began to focus on good things I began to have a different perspective on how I was seeing my life challenges. I decided to pick what was best. It was healthier and better for me to focus on good things instead of bad. I realized that when it comes to thinking good, I would always recall what the Bible says about the thinking. Proverbs 23:7 says, for as he thinketh in his heart so is he. In other words, we become what we think about. I had to take note that if I continued to think bad then I would become a negative person, and live my life from a negative point of view instead of being positive. It takes a lot of energy to be negative; and being positive did not require any energy at all. God did not ordain for me to live my life waking up and laying down and seeing my situations bad, but I knew God wanted me to see my situations changing from bad to good. The choice I realized was mine and at some point, I had to focus on the good instead of the bad. I realized that life was so much better now that I look at the good in my life's challenges. I could have chosen to live a depressing life of worrying about bad things all the time. No, I am at a new place in my life, and it feels so good. I want to be the best I can be by thinking about the good things that God has for me in my life. Now when I think about the bad things, I refocus and begin to think about what is true about my life.

How long does it take to refocus and think on good things instead of the bad? It does not take long at all. I figured it out by taking that bad thought and replacing it quickly with something good. For instance, if the doctor tells me my blood pressure was high. The way I would think was that it's high and may not come down. But God has taught me to focus on the good by saying even though the doctor says my blood pressure is high, I can do things to lower it and make it better. Now, this is good thinking; and this is the way I need and want to think.

Someone may ask why I would think like that in the first place. Because changing my way of thinking has been a process for me. I had to accept that thinking bad was not healthy for my mindset. Changing my mindset is good. But daily I must ask God to renew my mind and help me think with the power of God at work in me. I talk to God daily because changing my mindset could not be done on my own. I had to focus on having the mind of Christ. So, I would ask myself how Christ would tell me to think about my situation. I believe Christ would tell me to be positive and think good instead of bad.

I love this change in my life. It took many years and sharing with you to think good is better than thinking bad , and it is the key to becoming positive. I will get more out of life when I think about the good things and learn to deal with the negative situations from a positive standpoint. I always say to myself over and over; if I change my thinking then I can change my life.

Chapter 7

The dangers of having the wrong thinking mentality

I had to learn the hard way that possessing a negative attitude also created the wrong thinking mentality for me. I was living with a mindset that God did not design me to live with. I had chosen to let my past and the negative energy that come with it, define my future. Walking around day after day living my life from a mental standpoint of being negative about everything was draining the life not only out of me, but it was making my family feel very uncomfortable. I had the ability to be positive about my husband and children's life, hopes, and dreams, but I just could not be positive about myself or the things I had to accomplish. This was a dangerous way of visualizing and seeing myself. I would talk down about myself and would believe the worst. Being negative and allowing it to become a way of living for me was the cause of my depression and anxiety. I finally realize that I had enough of thinking like this.

What is a mentality? Merriam Webster Dictionary describes a mentality as a mode or way of thought, an Outlook. So, in other words, I need to focus on having a positive outlook about my life and situation. I realize there are times that life will come with struggles. I had to learn not to let what's going on around me affect what's in me. Being positive no matter is what should be showing up in my thoughts. My outlook on life needs to be good and not bad.

The dangers of having the wrong thinking mentality. The wrong thinking mentality can make you believe the worst about a situation. A wrong thinking mentality also causes us to have a lack of hope in our future. When the wrong thinking mentality takes over there is a strong possibility that depression and anxiety can set in about life. A wrong thinking mentality may often cause a lack of faith in God. A wrong thinking mentality can cause an individual to give up on living. One of the greatest dangers of a wrong thinking mind is that it causes one to worry all the time; and then it can affect your health. I know the dangers because I lived through them.

I began to realize that a wrong-thinking mentality was keeping me in a vicious cycle of going through the same thing over and over. I would encounter a situation and believe I would come out of it and believe that I did. Unfortunately, the same thing would come around again and instead of believing I had overcome it; I began to repeat that same situation with a defeated attitude. So, I realized I had to stop this cycle. This was affecting my relationship with God. I knew I needed to be delivered from this mentality and I knew I had to do something about it. You know I remember reading so many books about how to change the way I was seeing my life. God spoke to me one day and said, you can read the Bible and other books on how to change your mentality, but there must be applying what you are reading to your life.

I believe there are times in your life that you must be transparent to help other people. This is my truth, some years ago I struggled with having a positive mentality. Yes, I was preaching and pastoring people, but I realized then that I had some struggles. I loved helping other people and speaking victory over them, but I had to fight just to see myself living that victorious life. My eyes began to open, and I began to see that wrong thinking produces wrong living! I was not going to settle for living with this kind of outlook on life. One day I began crying out to God and requested that he deliver me from this type of mentality. I was preaching to others and telling them how to be free, but now I needed to be free. I can remember lifting my hands and saying God forgive me for my unbelief that I had walked with you, but I had not been dealing with my struggles. I asked the Lord to help me and give me peace and understanding that I was designed to have a God mentality. I noticed that things began to change in my life. I began to face things in my life that taught me compassion, to trust in God and that I could live in total victory. I felt a new mindset come over me. I began focusing on my spiritual self-care and making sure that I remembered that I have a right for renewal of mind to take place in my life via the power of the Holy Spirit. This was my time to embrace a new mindset and a new way of thinking.

Chapter 8

The power of a renewed mind

I truly believe that our minds can be changed if we allowed them to be. Negative thoughts can come from a negative place in our life. I learned this so well. The negative place in my life that the bad thoughts came from was my past. I knew that it would take God to help change the way I was thinking. My relationship with him was all I had to hold onto at times. At the deepest point of my depression, I had to learn to lean and depend on God to speak to my mind and remind me of how important I was to him. I knew at some point that I would have to allow God to deal with my mind in changing my thoughts from a negative to a positive. I needed God's help and I realized that doing this in my own strength would not work. I begin reading my Bible, and two of the most important scriptures to help me through my depression and anxiety was to continually be reading Ephesians 4:23-24th vs (NIV): To be made new in the attitude of your minds; and to put on the new self, created to be like God in true righteousness and holiness. I read this verse and it helped me to understand that I had to allow the Holy Spirit to give me a new attitude in my mind; a new way of thinking and understanding situations in my life; and to walk in the new person that God has made me to be with the power of the God working in my life so I can truly be a true representation of what it looks like when God changes your way of thinking. This is my truth; that having a renewed mind truly helped me to understand and see things the way God wants me to see them. God does not want my thinking to be reduced to thinking wrong about my life because HE has great plans for me. God wanted me to be planted strongly in him. I realized that I had to take on the mind of Christ. The Bible says in 1 Corinthians 2:16 vs. (Amplified version) For Who has known the mind and purposes of Lord, to instruct him? But we have the mind of Christ (to be guided by his thoughts and purposes). In other words, when I have the mind of Christ I can think right. I so agree with this. I had begun to say I have the mind of God in every area of my life and when things come up, I will think right about it. I know for sure that the power of the Holy Spirit working in my life has changed my way of thinking; and now I have a renewed mind. Being renewed in the mind has a lot to do with being positive. The renewed mind brings on a new mindset; a new mindset can help anyone see life from a different perspective. I see myself handling life's issues so much better. God has a way of making life even more pleasant. I feel so good because since I have changed my way of thinking, I have changed my way of living. In any area of life, it is so important to ask God to keep you with a renewed mind; so, day by day you will see life from a good place and continue to let the right thoughts catapult you to that new dimension of thinking. I am in a good space in my life. I continually see things from a positive perspective; and no matter how bad it gets I have learned that God is in control of my life. I have learned to pray and believe in God for a good outcome. I don't receive anything negative from anyone and I have learned to think positive. I am very careful what I allow individuals to speak into my life. I realized that part of operating in my new mindset of being positive is to be purposeful about what I let people speak into my life. Words are powerful and when something negative is spoken into my life, I rethink it and decide that I will not receive it. I have made a choice to make connections with positive people. I did not only change my way of thinking, but I had to use my voice and inform people that I was not going to allow anyone to speak negative to me concerning my life. I feel so much better. It's been many years that I have changed my mentality, and I do admit that my granddaughter was one of the chief reasons I changed not only my life but the way I was thinking. I will always be grateful for the change that has taken place in my life.

Chapter 9

A New Way of Thinking

I was so excited that life had changed for me. I was not the same person and my mentality had totally changed. I had developed a new way of thinking and it really felt so good. I had learned that everyone has a right to think the way they want to think. I had made up in my mind that I wanted to think right instead of wrong. When I was thinking wrong, I entertained a lot of negative thoughts and that was not a good idea. It was not a good idea because my thoughts made me look at every situation in my life as not having a good outcome.

My new way of thinking had made me realize I could get up and have a good day not matter what I was going to face because I was facing my day with God. My everyday life was turning into something I really enjoyed. I woke up excited about the plans I had for today; and that everything I put my hands to I could call it blessed. Every business decision I had to make was going to turn out well. I knew that work was going to be successful because I was going to work looking at every project I had to complete as turning out good. I went to visit my family and I was very positive; the family had fun we played games no disagreements. I also went to work and was no longer paranoid about people talking about me behind my back. All I know is that every encounter in my life was pictured from the point of being positive. This was a major change, and I was feeling very good about it. I was in a good space with my thinking and now I can focus on a new mentality when it comes to my thoughts.

My life has changed so much, and I am so appreciative of what God has done for me. I wake up every morning and lay down every night with the right kind of thinking. I like thinking right because it has helped my judgment; and I don't accept anything negative. I speak "life" over myself, and everything attached to me. When you change your way of thinking life is so much better. I not only change my way of thinking, but I do not entertain negative talk. I truly learned that positive thinking produces a positive life. It so good to feel this way.

Once I changed my way of thinking, I sat down and planned my day from beginning to end, by making sure my life was lining up with my thinking.

CHAPTER 10

I am Positive

I get up every morning excited about my day and the first thing I say to myself is "I AM POSITIVE! When I get up and command my day by saying I am positive, I am preparing myself to look at my day as great. I don't try to figure my day; I have learned to just live my day out. I pray to God every morning and I realize that he has my life in His hands. I have learned to give my day to God. I know what I must do, but I don't always know what I will face. I have learned to trust God and know that he knows what's best for me. I made the choice to think positive no matter what comes my way. I have learned to speak the opposite of what it looks like. You have a right to live with expectation and excitement of things changing for you. I live like that now. I don't accept defeat, so I have a determination to live a victorious life by being ready to make the necessary changes I need to make for a better day. I plan to make an impact in my own life but affirming myself to be the best I can be no matter what the situation. God has given me the power to make the right decision when issues arise because I have asked God to give me wisdom in every situation. I don't fly by the seat of my pants; I take what I have learned about life and mix it with a positive view, and everything turns out for my God. I am positive that I am walking in success. I can only be successful as I chose to be. Therefore, I stay positive because I am in a place in my life where I want to accomplish and fulfill my life dreams. I have learned that I must consistently be positive. I have to say continually I am a winner. All I do is win because I put God first in my life and I am focused on doing and being the best. I am positive that I will be fulfilling my God-given purpose because I stay right on track with what God tells me to do. I am positive that I am growing and that I want more out of life. I am positive that I am living my best life now. I am positive that I have overcome so many hurdles because I learned lessons that have made me want to do better. I am positive that thinking right is one of the best things I can do. I am positive that I have changed, and I am no longer the same, I want more out of life. I am positive that I love my life. I am positive that I have a renewed mind and that God helps me to think positive. I am positive that I will motivate other people to think positive about themselves and their life. I am positive that I will continue to achieve as many goals as possible; and that I will achieve them. I am positive that I will enjoy my life and I am so excited to be alive. I am positive that I will spend more time laughing at funny stuff. I am positively positive about going forward with a new perspective on my life. Lastly, I am going to be positive at living my best life now because I AM POSITIVE!

I had to make the choice to change my way of thinking and walk on the positive side. I wanted to write this book because I want to be transparent and share my journey to overcoming having a negative mentality. I want the readers to know and understand it doesn't matter what your status is in life everyone has struggles and wants to change something. I had to make some major changes and change my thinking to get the best out of life. You are worthy of God's love and so am I. Now when I get up in the morning, I see life so different. I get up ready for the day and what it holds for me. I always speak that my day is going to be good, and things are turning out in my favor! I don't' except doom and gloom! I used to wake up and be sad and depression had gripped me. Now, God has healed me, and I see myself healed in my mind, emotions and I operate totally in the mind of GOD. My mind is renewed, energized, reset, and bubbling over with positive thoughts. I want you to encourage to embrace your new way of thinking. I am not ashamed to share my transparency with the world. God healed me when I was going through several overwhelming periods in my life. I couldn't sleep and sometimes I didn't want to wake up. But you got to believe that God will heal your brokenness and perform his greatness towards you. You and I deserve to bet the best, live the best and maximize our fullest potential. I am so excited for the days to come. I have learned to appreciate and love my family and friends. I have come a long way, and I am so proud of myself. God brought me out and delivered me and now I attribute all the changes made in my life to God's power. I am in love with God, and I thank Him for bringing me this far. So now I share my truth that, "I AM POSITIVE!"

Chapter 11

Daily Affirmations About Being Positive

- I will not sweat the small stuff
- I was born with a purpose
- I can do it if I put my mind to it
- My feelings will not govern my emotions
- I am somebody
- I was born for this
- I will not compare myself to other people
- I am good enough
- I am whole and complete
- I refuse to give up
- I deserve the best
- I am a good person
- I am going to make my family proud
- I will not complain

- I will learn how to communicate better
- I am unstoppable
- I am a hard worker
- I am worthy
- I forgive myself
- I choose to be hopeful
- I am confident
- I am energetic
- I have a dream
- I have a story
- I am healing
- I will have a positive mindset
- I am allowed to feel good about myself
- I am better
- I am content
- I am optimistic
- I feel safe
- I am comfortable
- I am not judgmental
- I can breathe
- I have a good attitude

- I am growing
- I am an overcomer
- I am teachable
- I know how to let go of things
- I will allow myself to evolve and be what God wants me to be
- I am sensitive to God!
- I am blessed
- I am prosperous
- I am happy and joyful
- I am worthy to be loved
- I am not selfish
- I am understanding
- I am humble
- I am sure
- I am generous
- I feel healthy
- I am strong today
- I am patient and calm
- I am not distracted
- I can do anything I put my mind too

- I don't entertain negativity in any form or shape
- I am blessed to have a wonderful family and friends
- I am loved by my husband
- I am loved by my children
- I am a good mother
- I am a good Pastor
- I am a good sister
- I am a good daughter
- I believe in my dreams
- I am tough but resilient
- I am free
- I am integral
- I am motivated
- I am not my mistakes
- I choose to say no when I need to
- I choose to say yes when I want to
- I will prioritize my needs
- I know I will do what is right
- I know I am in God's hand
- I know being angry only hurts me

- The world is much better with me in it
- I deserve to be around people that love and respect me
- I radiate positivity
- My mind is calm
- I am amazing
- I treat my body well
- I believe in myself
- I take it easy

(These are some of the Affirmations I live by daily and they have made my life better.)

ABOUT THE AUTHOR

Antoinette Denise Upchurch is the Co-Founder and Senior Pastor of Increasing Faith Deliverance ministries along with her husband Overseer and Founder, Bishop Ulysses Upchurch in the city of Sanford, North Carolina.

Antoinette Denise Upchurch is a native of Sanford, North Carolina. Antoinette has overcome many challenges in life, as well as going through overwhelming times with her mental health, but God healed her and brought her out. Antoinette Upchurch has a Batchelor's Degree in Substance Abuse Counseling and a Master's Degree in Addiction Counseling with both degrees minoring in counseling. After overcoming overwhelming times in her mental health Antoinette decided to encourage people worldwide that they can overcome anything and to focus on being positive. Antoinette also has a Facebook Page called Walking with Denise that is designed to motivate, educate, and share information that can encourage people to live their best lives now and that God has designed for them to focus on being positive about their life.

Antoinette Denise Upchurch is also the author of God's Little Sunshine, and that book was designed to encourage families to continue being the best support system for their loved ones that have family members that are disabled.

Antoinette Denise Upchurch desires to see children, women, and men lives changed by them overcoming their struggles and focus on keeping a positive attitude about themselves.

Antoinette Denise Upchurch has a wonderful husband that she has been married to over 32 years; three beautiful adult children and a daughter and son-in-law and in-laws; and her son's girlfriend that she loves dearly, Antoinette also holds dear to her heart a mother, father, sister, and two brothers and sister-in-law, 2 nieces and several nephews, aunts, cousins, Godchildren, church family, friends, and co-laborers in Christ that she loves dearly: along with her beloved deceased granddaughter and mother-in-law.

www.ingramcontent.com/pod-product-compliance
Lightning Source LLC
LaVergne TN
LVHW051205080426
835508LV00021B/2825